Jupiter in Taurus 2023-2024

Predictions for your Zodiac Sign

Alina Rubi and Angeline Rubi

Published independently.

Copyright © 2023

Authors: Angeline Rubi and Alina A. Rubi

Email: rubiediciones29@gmail.com

No part of this book may be reproduced or transmitted in any form or by any electronic or mechanical means. Including photocopying, recording, or any other system of archiving and retrieving information, without the prior written permission of the author.

Introduction	5
Who is Aries?	15
What does Aries mean?	16
Mars, The Ruling Planet of Aries	17
Predictions for Aries	18
Who is Taurus?	24
What does Taurus mean?	25
Venus, The Ruling Planet of Taurus	26
Predictions for Taurus	26
Who is Gemini?	33
What does Gemini mean?	34
Mercury, the ruling planet of Gemini	35
Predictions for Gemini	35
Who is Cancer?	42
What does Cancer mean?	43
The Moon, The Ruling Planet of Cancer	44
Cancer Predictions	44
Who is Leo?	50
What does Leo mean?	51
The Sun, Leo's Ruling Planet	52
Predictions for Leo	52
Who is Virgo?	59
What does Virgo mean?	60
Mercury, The Ruling Planet of Virgo	60
Predictions for Virgo	61

Who is Libra?	68
What does Libra mean?	69
Venus, The Ruling Planet of Taurus	69
Predictions for Libra	70
Who is Scorpio?	76
What does Scorpio mean?	77
Pluto, The Ruling Planet of Scorpio	78
Predictions for Scorpio	78
Who is Sagittarius?	85
What does Sagittarius mean?	86
Jupiter, the ruling planet of Sagittarius	87
Predictions for Sagittarius	87
Who is Capricorn?	94
What does Capricorn mean?	95
Predictions for Capricorn	96
Who is Aquarius?	104
What does Aquarius mean?	105
Uranus, The Ruling Planet of Aquarius	106
Predictions for Aquarius	106
Who is Pisces?	113
What does Pisces mean?	114
Neptune, The Ruling Planet of Pisces	115
Predictions for Pisces	115
About the Authors	123

Introduction

On May 16, Jupiter transits to the sign of Taurus, where it will remain until May 26, 2024. On its journey through Taurus, Jupiter will guide us to focus on the structures we have built and check whether the environment we create allows us to thrive or survive.

Jupiter in Taurus will also evaluate topics related to pleasure, romance, and finances. During its transit through Taurus, Jupiter will make two extraordinarily revealing alignments, join the North Node, and towards the end of its march, join Uranus, releasing some magical energies.

Taurus is ruled by Venus, and is related to money, abundance, fertility, environment, self-esteem, and indulgence.

Jupiter is the planet of expansion, and during its stay on Taurus it will promote and dilate these issues.

The presence of Jupiter in this sign will make us concentrate on these areas of our lives and help us to obtain more utilities from them.

Jupiter is frequently considered the providential planet, as it helps us focus on the positives, can expand our minds, bringing new opportunities, ideas, and deeper knowledge.

Jupiter in Taurus does not act hastily, so any change brought about by this astral flow will work best when there is a systematic and organized organization, when you adopt a step-by-step perspective and do not act with haste. That is, if you are slow and persistent you will get many benefits.

Jupiter in Taurus can sometimes create a heavy energy that makes it easy to become sloppy and lazy or postpone what we want to do. But one of the gifts that Taurus offers us is to slow down, reflect on what is important and be available to stop and think.

Problems only occur when we become imprisoned in this state to the point that we run out of direction and lose our aspirations.

Finding time to rest, enjoy and play is always exciting, but with Jupiter in Taurus, we may have to be wise not to overdo it.

Jupiter in Taurus will guide us to think about the contexts we have created for ourselves and whether they are affirming not only our dreams and goals, but also our nervous system.

Over the past 12 months, as Jupiter crossed Aries, he led us to plant seeds, undertake new things, and take some leaps of faith. But now, once he moves to Taurus, he wants us to sow the seeds that really matter and make sure the environment is figured so they can thrive.

Creating a positive environment is something we can exploit as Jupiter travels through Taurus. If you're not happy with your life, work environment, or even the environments you've created in your relationships, this is the perfect time to make a transformation.

With this transit we will focus our attention on the state of our planet and how we choose to exploit or abuse its resources. Taurus is connected to agronomy and livestock, Jupiter is the planet of expansion, so while it can bring greater awareness about the ways we can care for and safeguard our planet, it can also bring an expansion of projects that do the reverse.

The energy is there for us to use, it's just up to us to use it in the right direction.

Jupiter in Taurus is also all about money issues as both are connected to wealth, so this could be an ideal time to expand your wealth and personal resources. However, Jupiter and Taurus can also be connected to a lot of responsibilities, obligations, and difficulties, but anyway Jupiter's entry into Taurus is a good opportunity to get your finances in order, not only evaluate and pay debts, but also do business, purchases, and speculations.

Investing your money can feel a bit threatening, but learning to trade with ease is a great way to use this Jupiter energy in Taurus, of course having a wide range of investments is a good idea, but if you don't have extra money, you can also create abundance in other areas, such as: growing your own food, develop new faculties or choose a substitute or alternate job.

Focusing on a fertile mindset and knowing your value are also ways to create wealth, and having an abundant mindset is not just about thinking positive, it's about thinking with an open mind, that is, instead of being locked into an inflexible mindset, if you maintain some openness, more opportunities will appear in your life.

A limited mindset is often based on putting up excuses and reasons why something can't be done, but an abundant mindset asks: - why not? - and focuses on what is possible.

Jupiter in Taurus also carries a seal for indulgence especially in things like food and travel. While we shouldn't live beyond our means, this could be a novelesque and wonderful time to take that international trip or splurge on a first-class restaurant.

Choosing an international destination based on food and civilization or taking a food tour can also be a fantastic way to work with this energy, but something wiser would be to sign up for a wine or cooking class.

In other words, think about what brings you pleasure and try to infiltrate your daily life because Jupiter in Taurus guides us to focus on both the great and simple delights.

Give yourself enough to make it feel like something special, but don't stand out.

As Jupiter transits Taurus, it will align with the North Node, making its energy enormously strong, and we will feel this most powerfully during May and the entire month of June 2023.

The North Node symbolizes our collective destiny and where we are headed, it is like the compass of the planet, and the direction in which we are being stimulated to go.

The North Node has been on Taurus since January 2022 and is slowly changing, but this final union with Jupiter will expand its themes.

Jupiter and the North Node when coupled can precipitate events, that is, things that we speculated were on the horizon or – for the future – may arrive unexpectedly at our doorstep.

The union of Jupiter and the North Node is truly an unlikely and special once-in-a-lifetime event and shows that whatever unfolds in the next 12 months will be decisive in the direction we are headed towards as humanity.

Jupiter will also make an incredible alignment with the planet Uranus. This energy will be more active between April and May 2024, when Jupiter prepares to leave Taurus.

Uranus is the planet of awakening, change and innovation, he wants us to fragment borders, seek greater freedom and do things our way.

The union of Uranus and Jupiter in Taurus could bring some volatility or grandiose changes in areas related to agriculture, business, and economies, and could bring an acceleration of transformative technology such as AI or even digital currencies.

Jupiter is the happiest of all the planets, it has the popularity of bringing good luck and wealth. With Jupiter we can not only expand our wealth, but also our minds. This planet is related to the higher mind, philosophy, and religion, and always offers us the opportunity to see the world through a clear and clean lens.

Jupiter drives thought, and Taurus is the most static sign. When they are coupled, they remind us that the solutions we ask for are within us. Spirituality is always present within us, but with the distractions of daily life we easily ignore it. With this transit, we are given the opportunity to overcome those distractions and benefit from the natural wisdom that has always been hidden within us.

There is a relaxing sensation, but at the same time restricted when Jupiter the exaggerated moves towards the practical Taurus. Jupiter is always ready to enlarge, but Taurus tends to add immobility to this astral combination. Jupiter has general goals, but Taurus delays things at a more objective and balanced pace.

If we use these energies correctly there is no reason to be discouraged, as Jupiter in Taurus is the perfect occasion to really make our dreams come true, or a long-term purpose. During this period, we have the desire for expansion of Jupiter, and the patience and endurance of Taurus. This motivates us to believe in our projects and achieve success. Our lives can be extremely prosperous during the transit of

Jupiter through Taurus, since Taurus rules wealth and Jupiter good luck. This combination can result in us analyzing our economic situation and looking for growth opportunities.

It is especially important to be responsible during this transit because the negative side of Taurus is that it likes pleasure and indulgence, and when a planet as expansive as Jupiter comes into relationship with a sign that exaggerates pleasure, we can confuse our needs with whims. We must make a commitment to be patient and careful with our desires during this transit.

When the effusive Jupiter transits retrograde through Taurus, we will feel its part firm and withdrawn. When Jupiter moves backwards in its retrograde span, we are encouraged to slow down and ask ourselves what are we, where are we, and where are we going?

Therefore, during the time that Jupiter is retrograde in Taurus, we will be analyzing and evaluating our goals, and reflecting if the projects in which we want to invest the time are appropriate for us, and if we are doing it correctly. Is the result going to make you feel happy and fulfilled? This question is difficult, but the answer is decisive. The retrograde transit of Jupiter through Taurus is the perfect opportunity to clarify and strengthen our objectives, in this way we will find a reasonable, and safe, path before moving forward.

Who is Aries?

Dates: March 21 – April 19

Day: Tuesday

Color: Red

Element: Fire

Compatibility: Leo, Libra, Sagittarius, and Aquarius

Symbol: ♈

Element: Fire

Modality: Cardinal

Polarity: Male

Ruling planet: Mars

House: 1

Metal: Iron, steel

Quartz: Red Jasper, Ruby

Constellation: Aries

What does Aries mean?

Aries is a Latin term 'arietis', which since ancient times has meant 'Aries', according to Pliny (first century AD), Aries was also a certain type of sea monster extremely dangerous for boats. Likewise, it was a military machine to knock down walls because it worked by ramming, like the Aries.

Aries is the first zodiac sign, it is associated with Spring, it is the symbol of rebirth and beginnings. It belongs to the cardinal signs, those that coincide with the change of season along with Cancer, Libra, and Capricorn.

There is also a link between Aries and Ares, the fearsome god of war.

Mars, The Ruling Planet of Aries

Mars gives Aries the personality of a leader, strategist, and planner with great intelligence. It will always be the first to promote the fight against injustices. His words are definitive in any discussion. They get upset very easily, although they are not spiteful.

The energy of the planet Mars has great power over this zodiac sign.

This planet, named by the Greeks in honor of the god Ares, gives rise to the name of this zodiac sign, in addition to providing curious details about the personality of the Aries.

Those born by this sign, sometimes, the bad temper comes out automatically. This does not define them totally, and it is common to find sweet and laughing Arians with whom to share joyful moments.

However, when an Aries has an unstable and bellicose personality, anything can explode.

Predictions for Aries

Aries, Jupiter has just left your sign, leaving you in one of the most advantageous positions. Now you're in a position where you can take everything you learned, all those possibilities and all those things that expanded, and choose what you want to focus on.

This is your time to nurture the opportunities you really want and to narrow your focus. You planted a lot of seeds while Jupiter was touring your sign, but now it's time to pay attention to the ones that will bear the most fruit, or the ones that really matter to you.

Now you can go out into the world with this new way of thinking, more grounded and integrated into your being and this can allow you to see things in a new way and approach them in a different way than you had before. People around you may comment that some of your beliefs or even values have changed, but this is only because Jupiter has guided your expansion into a new way of being. As Jupiter has just left your sign, it can also be a good time to reflect on any opportunities that have come your way.

In addition to reaping the benefits of the cosmic dust Jupiter left in your sign, you also have some new energies to work with. Jupiter will now move to the part of your chart that deals with money, finances, and self-esteem, all of which are intertwined.

While Jupiter in Taurus is a good time to clarify money matters in general, this is especially true for you. This is a time of power to make sure your value is recognized, especially when it comes to your job or income.

Use this energy to be confident and ask for a raise, to enforce your terms and conditions, or even to ask for a higher title. If you feel like you're being passed over or taken advantage of in your current job, here's your chance to make some changes.

Just remember to master your impulses, because when working with Taurus energy, the best approach is slow, methodical steps.

Do your research and give reasons to back up what you're asking for, be firm in what you want, assert yourself, and have a backup plan in case things don't.

Visualize what you want, if you decide to leave your current workplace, and seek a higher position than you have now, Jupiter in Taurus will guide you along the way.

With Jupiter moving through Taurus, you also have some of the best energies for wealth creation, if your income isn't going to move anytime soon, you could explore the possibility of choosing a side job or exercising your creative talents and going for something a little more entrepreneurial.

There are fantastic creative energies flowing from the cosmic skies for you, and if you involve technology in any way, it could be doubly lucrative. Take the opportunity if there's something you want to do, start that podcast, sell that digital art, or sell your homemade products online or through social media. Having Jupiter in your sign should have started a creative impulse within you, so this is your chance to build a solid foundation and have more structure and stability around your income.

Something you should keep in mind when Jupiter arrives in this corner of the cosmic sky is your expenses. They can tend to go up, so keep this in mind, don't make unnecessary purchases and do your best to keep start-up costs low if you plan on doing something businesslike.

This wouldn't be a good year to lend people money or take a big financial risk on something you don't feel confident about. Of course, follow your instincts, but be incredibly careful when approaching this kind of thing.

Jupiter in Taurus may bring some unexpected expenses, or something may cost more than you thought, so keep this in mind and try to minimize any frivolous expenses. If you have a big expense to make this year, like a wedding or buying a house, you can go ahead with it, but have a solid plan for how you're going to make payments. Taurus is all about taking a step-by-step approach so you can create a solid foundation overall.

So, keep this mindset and see how everything fits perfectly into place.

On an intuitive level, the shift from Jupiter to Taurus will highlight all the ways you need to love yourself more deeply. Since your Aries are so fiery, sometimes it's hard for you to stick to a path.

Sometimes you may find yourself chasing new experiences or new beginnings, like an addictive impulse or habit. Sometimes, just as you are about to reach the true depth of something, you decide to turn and walk in a new direction.

If you resonate with any of this, this is your chance to become aware of what drives these impulses. You may want to challenge yourself and see if you can follow up with something and pull it off to break that habit or pattern. In the end Taurus is a very earthly and ingrained energy, so you have this on your side to use! Aries, this is an opportunity for you to not only plant the seed but stay with it long enough to see how the seed blooms.

Who is Taurus?

Dates: April 20 -May 21

Day: Friday

Color: Green

Element: Earth

Compatibility: Cancer, Virgo, Scorpio, Capricorn

Symbol: ♉

Modality: Fixed

Polarity: Feminine

Ruling planet: Venus

House: 2

Metal: Copper

Quartz: Rose Quartz, Emerald

Constellation: Taurus

What does Taurus mean?

In mythology Cerus was a wandering, hermit, and wild bull, who had no owner. One day, Persephone, the goddess of spring, found him mistreating the flowers and approached him. The beauty and kindness of the young woman reassured him, and the animal fell totally in love with her. Persephone tamed and tamed Cerus, educated and instructed him to be patient and to use his strength with talent.

In the Fall, when Persephone went to Hades, Cerus went to heaven and transformed into the constellation Taurus. Every year, when spring comes, Persephone returns to Earth and Cerus joins her. In that period the goddess rides on her back, walks through the fields bathed in sun, and makes all the plants and flowers sprout.

Venus, The Ruling Planet of Taurus

Venus is the Goddess of Love. Venus rules the signs of Libra and Taurus. Venus is related to two main areas of our life: love and money. Love and Money really is a simplistic interpretation of Venus. Venus rules what we value, and the pleasure of life. Grace, charm, and beauty are ruled by Venus. Through Venus, we can know our tastes, pleasures, artistic inclinations, and the things that make us happy.

Predictions for Taurus

Taurus, con Jupiter in your sign, you are the protagonist of the zodiac. This is an exciting opportunity to take Jupiter's energy and apply it to all areas of your life.

Jupiter is the planet of expansion and abundance, so think of an area of your life you'd like to expand and channel Jupiter's magic in that direction.

Jupiter is considered the lucky planet; it helps us focus on the positives and makes it easier for us to focus on a positive mindset.

This will be a welcome thing for you, Taurus, as you have been receiving significant training over the past few years.

Since 2018, you have had Uranus, the planet of change, moving through your sign. Uranus brings volatile energy, helping to shake things in our lives that are no longer stable or that are no longer supporting the true essence of our soul.

Uranus calls us to have more freedom, to free ourselves from social or infantile conditioning and enter a more authentic version of ourselves. While the result is worth it, there's a struggle along the way, and you've been feeling that.

To add a little more to all this, the Eclipse has also been falling into your sign, with one more to come in October 2023. Having the Eclipses in your sign means that you have been feeling the weight of transformative energies. Your life is likely to look completely different than it did in 2018.

Take a moment to celebrate all the ways you've changed and all the growth you've moved through. Especially honor any point of independence or freedom you have created by stepping into your true, authentic self.

The presence of Jupiter in your sign will be welcome, however, it is a lot of energy to navigate, and with Uranus here too, it could sometimes feel very overwhelming. Of all the zodiac signs, you're one of the best at grounding and focusing your energy, so come back to this when you need to.

Be sure to take it easy, catch your breath, and stay as present as possible as you navigate through any turmoil.

Change can always disperse our energy, so be kind to yourself and focus on taking small steps forward. You may not yet be able to see the full road ahead, but small steps will get you there at the perfect time.

Jupiter in your sign can also speed things up, which means that, if changes have been in process, it's possible for things to move a little faster now. This might be a welcome thing, especially if you've been feeling a little stuck. However, it could also increase the burden, making you feel like you're playing catch-up, Jupiter is a positive force, but it comes with its little dangers to navigate.

As Jupiter approaches Uranus in 2024, you may start to see some rewards and abundance blossoming in your life. In fact, this is a wonderful opportunity to create more abundance for yourself, especially if you find yourself in a new territory.

If the changes take place in early 2024, they are likely to be very plentiful and bring a lot of success in their own way. You can harness this energy by making positive changes in your life during this window of time. These changes can be as bold as you want them to be. In fact, Uranus, and Jupiter together, especially in early 2024, will encourage you to be innovative, to do something out of the ordinary, to think freely, and to stretch your horizons.

The changes you make, big or small, will bring you opportunities and expansion for years to come. This will be a beautiful opportunity for you to set your sights high and go for what you want. Even if it seems a little daring or out of place, this energy is really on your side and can bring many opportunities for success.

Use this energy to your advantage. Taurus when Jupiter enters your sign, touches all areas of your life, helping to expand and raise awareness about the issues that need to be dealt with, your mind will be particularly vulnerable during this transit, which means you can learn fast and be more sensitive to new information.

When channeled in the right way, this can be excellent to expand your knowledge, increase your spiritual awareness and change your attitudes and beliefs, for example if you have wanted to study or go back to school, this is a fantastic energy that you have on your side since Jupiter, expands your mind in a new way, helping to break old beliefs and build new ones, but you have to be aware of allowing yourself to be brainwashed or allowing your mind to wander far into the depths even though it is difficult for you to be present in this physical reality.

Having your mind expanded is a wonderful thing and will allow you to free yourself from limitations, but it simply comes back to your heart and soul when it comes to determining what is truly true and what kind of thoughts you want to hold on to.

Your health can also stand out as Jupiter travels through your sign. Jupiter can bring healing, but it can also expand health problems you've ignored. While this sounds a little daunting, having things expanded allows us to act finally, and can help us make sense of any strange symptoms that are difficult to diagnose. In fact, if you've been struggling with some dark symptoms or just want your body to have optimal health, Jupiter will lend you its support and guide you to take the right steps.

Jupiter can be excessive at times, so keep this in mind on your wellness journey because while it's great to make healthy changes and find the underlying cause of things, you shouldn't let this become an unhealthy obsession. Jupiter in your sign, along with the presence of Uranus, is truly a special gift.

Success and abundance will follow you; Jupiter will bring the rewards and gifts of all your efforts, you will find that your mind expands in new ways, which will filter into your thoughts, your actions, and the way you communicate. So, my advice is to enjoy the trip.

Who is Gemini?

Dates: 21 May - 21 June

Day: Wednesday

Color: Blue

Element: Air

Compatibility: Libra, Aries, and Aquarius

Symbol: ♊

Modality: Mutable

Polarity: Male

Ruling planet: Mercury

House: 3

Metal: Mercury

Quartz: Crystal, beryl, and topaz.

Constellation: Gemini

What does Gemini mean?

There is a myth related to Gemini that tells that two brothers Castor and Pollux, sons of Zeus, lived united by an immense friendship. Beaver was mortal and Pollux, immortal. Cheerful, determined, and physically vital, the two brothers excelled equally on the fighting field.

The love caused the death of Castor, who kidnapped one of the daughters of Leucippus, with whom he was in love. Harassed and killed by the girl's boyfriend, he died in the fight. Pollux, dejected by the death of his brother, begged Zeus to grant him life again. Zeus failed to fully fulfill his request, but united the two brothers in the constellation Gemini so that they could both live together for eternity.

Mercury, the ruling planet of Gemini

Mercury, the messenger of the gods, is the planet that rules Gemini and Virgo. It is the planet of the
communication. The function of Mercury is to dismantle things and rebuild them. It is an emotionless and indiscreet planet.

Mercury not only rules communication but represents organization and tactics.
Ideas and sensory information need to be coordinated and organized. Mercury analyzes, It classifies groups and gives meaning to those ideas.

Predictions for Gemini

Gemini, Jupiter in Taurus is working in the deeper layers of your subconscious mind.

Jupiter, in this position, has been compared to a Guardian Angel working hard in your life. You may not even be aware that it is there, but it is supporting and guiding you from hidden realms, being subtle enough that you have no proof, but helpful enough to feel that something divine must be at stake.

Jupiter will be your Guardian Angel for the next year, taking care of you, but giving you the freedom of choice to go in the direction you want.

Jupiter will also work in your subconscious mind, pulling out some of those hidden thoughts, feelings, and beliefs so you can work through them finally.

Jupiter is the planet of expansion, so you may find yourself digging deep into your subconscious mind and eliminating what you no longer need and what still needs to be dealt with. Jupiter in this position can be fantastic to collaborate with a therapist or try other healing modalities such as hypnosis, past life regressions, or other trauma work.

Jupiter will increase your success and healing with these areas. You may also find yourself working behind the scenes on a project that is becoming incredibly lucrative.

You may not yet see how lucrative it is, but all the hard work you're doing behind the scenes will pay off when Jupiter moves into your sign in May 2024.

You must clean up the old, remove all subconscious barriers, and prepare your mind for the expansion that Jupiter will bring because when Jupiter enters your sign next year, it will bring expansion in all areas, and this expansion will allow you to nurture your dreams, seek opportunities, and connect with abundance.

Your job now is to clear the space a bit, identifying limiting beliefs and thoughts or behaviors that keep you stuck. Of course, this is difficult to do.

You cannot be aware of what you are not aware. But that's where Jupiter is going to help you. Jupiter will be your guide, helping you peel off the layers and face some of those skeletons in your closet. Think of it this way, Jupiter is working on the background of your life, as a writer of a story would.

The writer must go inward, enter the zone, and withdraw from the world to author his story. It's hard work and even isolating at times. But in those quiet moments, inspiration flows, magic happens when your fingers click on the keys.

And while all of this is happening privately, it won't be long before hundreds read the story, even millions. When Jupiter enters Gemini, that's when your story will be out there for the world to see.

You will no longer be working hard in your small office buried in your inspirations and thoughts; Your words will be in the world and will give you attention and success. This is a good analogy for where Jupiter is taking you, but since it's in Taurus, you're in the isolation phase, working on your story behind the scenes. Reflect on how this story fits into your life and where you are now. How do you get the idea of the writer working behind the scenes?

During this time, you can also begin to think about what you want to manifest and expand in your life. Remember, Jupiter is the planet of expansion, and when it moves into your sign, you will be in the prime place to receive that expansion. Use your time now to focus on what you want to expand.

Clear things out of your life to make room for that expansion. Prepare for it by setting your mindset in that direction.

We don't attract what we want in this life, we attract what we are. So, align yourself with your authentic truth and what feels right to you, and the rest will fall into place.

When Jupiter is near, we can often use its cosmic magic to bring more abundance and wealth into our lives. As your turn with Jupiter approaches, you can use this energy now to put your mindset in a more abundant place. This could include reciting affirmations and mantras, but it's about being abundant in all areas of thought.

Abundant thought is open to possibilities; Ask how things are possible, rather than making excuses. A good challenge you may want to set for yourself is to stop complaining.

Complaining can instantly drag us down and can feed a limited mindset. For the next 12 months, try not to complain.

This doesn't mean you can't have emotions or feelings but try to take the idea of complaining and turn it around. When something uncomfortable happens, rethink it. It's hard to do.

But it's a good challenge to create a more abundant mindset.

Another tip for creating an abundant mindset is to say yes to more things. Being positive opens us up to more opportunities and experiences. While they are not always the right experiences for us, who knows where they may take us? Experiment with these ideas and this will put you in a fantastic position once Jupiter moves into your sign, because Jupiter will help you take that mindset and run with it, allowing you to manifest things in your reality.

During the transit of Jupiter in Taurus, you may also feel restless. This restlessness can come from feeling uninspired, exhausted, or simply being in the wrong place.

As Jupiter approaches Uranus in 2024, this feeling may begin to become more apparent. It may require you to make some changes, Jupiter and Uranus will be intricately connected from April to May 2024, so that's when you can experience the worst part of any change.

If things feel unsettling right now, the best strategy is to be patient. Also, keep in mind that any changes you make during this window have the potential to bring you a lot of success. Just make sure you follow your intuition and listen to your own instincts. Jupiter in Taurus is a steppingstone to one of your best years.

Trust that your energy is preparing you for the successful chapter ahead.

Who is Cancer?

Dates: June 22 to July 22

Day: Monday

Color: White, Silver

Element: Water

Compatibility: Taurus, Pisces

Symbol:

Modality: Cardinal

Polarity: Feminine

Ruling planet: Moon

House: 4

Metal: Silver

Quartz: Moonstone, Pearl, Rose Quartz,

Constellation: Cancer

What does Cancer mean?

In mythology, Carcinos was a gigantic crab who watched over the ocean nymphs of Poseidon's reign. It was monumental and eternal. Completely devoted to his role as guardian.

One day, some nymphs fled and Carcinos sent a huge squid to look for them, but the squid decided to devour them instead of rescuing them.

When he returned, Carcinos did not forgive him and fought against him until he was dismembered. Injured and dying, he was rescued by Poseidon, who soothed his grief by placing him in the sky as the constellation of Cancer. This constellation reminds us of the protective nature of this sign, and its sensitivity.

The Moon, The Ruling Planet of Cancer

The Moon symbolizes our deepest intimate needs, our habits and reactions, and our subconscious.
The Moon is associated with the mother. The Moon is our inner child and our mother. It is sensitive,
Receptive, abstracted, and introspective. The Moon represents our automatic, intuitive, and involuntary reactions.

Cancer Predictions

For Cancer, well you've heard the saying: it's not what you know, but who you know, and this is exactly the mantra Jupiter has for you when it enters Taurus. Your networks are about to expand.

You might find yourself meeting new people, connecting with more like-minded souls, and being introduced to people who can take you further. Creating a community feels difficult in these modern times. Everyone is so busy with their own lives and schedules that it can be hard to take the time to create a sense of community in your life. But that's what you're being called to focus on as Jupiter moves through Taurus.

There have been a lot of changes in your circle of friends, or in the group of people you were once close to. Their values changed, you feel like you changed, and you just don't identify with some of their beliefs and values anymore.

Some friends are forever, and others are only for a season. Honoring this is important. It may be time to put aside certain relationships so that others more aligned can follow.

It may also be time to expose yourself so you can meet a new team. Jupiter in Taurus will help you with this, guiding you to set some boundaries and encouraging you to be more social.

Don't be discouraged if you've had setbacks with friendships or in building a community. You can change things, so stay positive and watch a strong community start to form around you.

To be clear, when I write community it's about having a group of friends who are your chosen family. I mean people you can lean on, trust, talk to, and have fun with.

You might have some people in your life like these, if so, you're lucky!

But Jupiter will help you create more similar connections.

To act on this energy, consider joining a group or club, or attending a networking event in your area. You never know who you might run into.

Loneliness is truly a silent killer, so if you feel that way, make a switch with Jupiter in Taurus.

Consider meeting new people and working to create a supportive community. If you're looking to get a boost in your career, you may be incredibly lucky to ask for help or advice from someone you admire or trust.

Sometimes just asking can open doors and pave the way to get where you want to be. As a Cancer, you can be sensitive and shy, and reaching out can be uncomfortable, but challenge yourself. Expose yourself and wait for the results.

You might get some pushback, and not everyone will like your idea or be willing to help, but you never know until you try.

As Jupiter moves through Taurus, it is also likely to bring you an opportunity for abundance through a friend or someone you know.

For you, networking would be a fantastic resource this year, but just being genuine and helping a partner can also open a path for you.

Jupiter in this location, can also expand your spiritual gifts and knowledge, you can be guided to learn more from spiritual experts and even certain religions.

Use this energy to open your mind and deepen your own personal spiritual connection. Through this deep spiritual connection, you may also find that Jupiter in Taurus inspires you to think about your dreams and goals in the future.

Jupiter in Taurus is guiding us all to create an environment in which we can thrive, and on this journey, you may find that some of your dreams and goals are no longer creating the prosperity you seek.

Life circumstances change, and sometimes we exceed the dreams and goals we once had. As Jupiter moves to align with Uranus from April to May 2024, you may find yourself changing paths or deciding to head in a different direction when it comes to your dreams and goals.

It can be sad to let go of a dream, especially if we never saw it come to fruition, but trust the ideas and awareness that Jupiter brings in Taurus because it is helping you create more abundance and more alignment in your life, so if something feels like it doesn't fit, trust and listen to that voice.

As you let go of the dream, you may wonder what's next, the path may still be unclear, and you may feel like you're in a period of limbo but be patient and trust the flow. You shouldn't have it all figured out. In fact, when Jupiter leaves Taurus and enters Gemini in May 2024, you will have much better cosmic support to think about what new dreams and goals you wish to manifest and pave the way.

In general, use this energy from Jupiter in Taurus to focus on building and expanding your networks and community. Reach out and lean on others for guidance, support, and advice.

On a deeper level, you'll find that some personal dreams and goals you were working towards are no longer conducive to creating an environment in which you can thrive, so trust these feelings and make room to let things go.

Who is Leo?

Dates: July 24 – August 23

Day: Sunday

Color: Yellow, Gold

Element: Fire

Compatibility: Aquarius, Sagittarius, Aries,

Symbol: ♌

Fixed Modality

Polarity: Male

Ruling planet: Sun

House 5

Metal: Gold.

Quartz: Ruby, diamonds, Onyx.

Constellation: Leo

What does Leo mean?

According to legends, Leo was a beast mystically popularly known as the Nemean Lion. He lived in a cave with two entrances where he spread terror in neighboring towns.

Hercules, son of Zeus, agreed to do twelve jobs, and one of them was to kill the Nemean Lion, a fact considered impossible for a mortal.

Hercules, knowing that the Lion was immune to weapons, managed to kill him with his bare hands, strangling him. Perceiving the powers of the Lion's skin, Hercules with the skin made a cloak and a helmet. After his defeat, the Lion was placed in the sky as the constellation of Leo, in honor of his divine power and supernatural forces.

The Sun, Leo's Ruling Planet

The Sun represents our ego, it is the part of us that makes the decisions. The Sun is our identity, and
general vitality.
The Sun is considered the head of our natal chart, and he shows what we are learning to be.

Predictions for Leo

For Leo, Jupiter moving into Taurus makes Taurus the star of the zodiac, but you follow him.

You have Jupiter in a prime position to receive abundance, success, and even fame. This is your chance to see your name in the lights, to strive higher, and go for your dreams and goals.

If you've ever wanted to make a career change, this is your chance to do so. Dream big as I always say, aim high and see what you can manifest under this alignment, as the sky is really the limit!

You have some of the best energy to get where you want, not only in your career, but also in your purposes. Even if you're retired or not interested in pushing your profession forward, this alignment can help enrich your life, allowing you to wake up every morning and feel satisfied with what you're doing.

The first step with this is to be clear about what you want. How do you want to wake up and feel every morning? What things make you feel that way? What brings you satisfaction?

All these questions are fuels to help you tap into the waves of cosmic juice Jupiter is leaving you. You must be clear about your goals and dreams and start taking steps to make them a reality.

With Jupiter in Taurus, these steps need to be small and methodical, it's not just about jumping in and hoping there's a network, this energy is about being planned, making sure the grid is in place and creating a solid foundation.

You may have big dreams and visions, but this energy requires you to create a solid platform for them to stand too. One exercise you should try is one called a reverse chessboard. In this exercise, you think about your end goal and where you want to be.

Then you trace your steps back one by one to get to where you are today. For example, if your goal is to author a book and make it a bestseller, a step back from this would be to start writing it.

The step back from that would be to think of a theme for this book and so on. Of course, you must be more detailed than I have been here; It really breaks down each step-in detail until you get to where you are today.

The smaller you take each step, the easier it will be to chart a path to get to where you want to be. This is just an exercise to help you create a solid foundation, but of course, you can follow your own rhythms and ideas. If you're currently employed and want to stay where you are, you can also use this energy to ask for a raise, get a promotion, or take on a new project.

There's professional success all around you, so hopefully, you can put it to good use and get where you want to be. When it comes to feeling more in tune with your purpose, it's helpful to remember that your purpose isn't something you get from the outside but rather, from the inside.

I know that certain activities can give us a greater sense of purpose, but our true purpose, our higher purpose really comes from within. It is something we find in the meaning of all things, not just when we are doing what we love to do.

Emotions can grow and give up, but our feelings of purpose are always there when we put ourselves in a state of true alignment. Feeling purposeful is about giving meaning to your life. It's about making the most of your time here and being present at every moment.

What is the purpose of this human life? We must live deeply so that time here is not wasted. We should not wait to answer this question. The quality of our life depends on how deeply we live each moment and not on emotional and material comforts.

Believe me that money, power, and prestige may not provide this quality or happiness.

Meditate on these words and see what they inspire in you, but don't forget that part of your mission in this life is to spend time growing, learning, failing, succeeding, exploring, and having fun.

All these states can lead you to discover a deeper connection with yourself and, consequently, help you feel more in tune with your purpose.

With so much potential for success under this alignment, it's also important to remember to stay grounded. Taurus is a deep-rooted energy, and we are being guided to be methodical and practical in our approach. However, Taurus energy can also be very forgiving, enjoying the pleasures that life can bring. Keep this in mind.

Enjoy any success that comes your way, but make sure you don't overdo things or become excessive.

You may also need to keep your ego in check, to make sure you stay balanced. If you notice your ego rising, breathe in and imagine the energy moving from your head to your lower body.

As the energy moves from your hot head into your body, it has a cooling and grounding effect, helping you think more clearly and focus on what is enormously important in your heart.

Finally, Leoncito, as Jupiter prepares to conclude its journey in Taurus, will align with Uranus from April to May 2024, adding a tinge of instability. There could be some volatility right now, which could bring sudden changes to your workplace or profession.

You may receive a stroke of inspiration to evaluate the waters of a new path, or you may find that something fades away. While change can always be difficult at first, Jupiter's presence promises that abundance will follow!

Also, remember that if something ends abruptly right now, it's only paving the way for something new and more abundant to emerge.

You have some of the brightest energies to expand your career and purpose. Success, abundance, and fame are on your side, so put them to work.

Take steps to activate this energy in your life and make it a reality. Jupiter only reaches this position on your chart once every 12 years, enjoy it.

Who is Virgo?

Dates: August 23 - September 22

Day: Wednesday

Color: Brown

Element: Earth

Compatibility: Capricorn, Pisces, Taurus, and Cancer

Symbol: ♍

Modality: Mutable

Polarity: Feminine

Ruling planet: Mercury

House: 6 (health and service)

Metal: Mercury

Quartz: sapphire, carnelian, and amazonite.

Constellation: Virgo

What does Virgo mean?

When Pandora could not resist the urge to open the box with the famous name, she cast a curse on humans, and the gods left Earth and went to live in heaven.

Astrea, deity of justice, innocence, and purity, afflicted with the misery, war and coldness of humans with their responsibilities to the divine deities, was the last to leave, sheltering in the constellation of Virgo.

The scale of Astrea is also part of the constellation of Libra, reminding humans of the value of justice. The constellation of Virgo represents the justice that must prevail in the world.

Mercury, The Ruling Planet of Virgo

Mercury, the messenger of the gods, is the planet that rules Gemini and Virgo. It is the planet of communication. The function of

Mercury is to dismantle things and rebuild them. It is an emotionless and indiscreet planet.

Mercury not only rules communication but represents organization and tactics.

Ideas and sensory information need to be coordinated and organized. Mercury analyzes, classifies, groups, and makes sense of those ideas.

Predictions for Virgo

Your Virgo, you will truly benefit from this energy and see your life expand in bright and inspiring ways.

First, Jupiter is illuminating the part of your chart connected to international travel, if you have always dreamed of making that trip abroad, this may be your time to do so. Jupiter will ensure that the journey is magical, and breathtaking. In fact, if you're looking for love or craving inspiration, this trip is likely to bring it to you.

There's a lot of positive energy to absorb here, so if it's a possibility, take steps to make it happen.

You are a grounded and organized Virgo, so there may be no need to say this, but when it comes to Taurus energy, it is important to be methodical and take practical steps to achieve your goals.

So, when it comes to any trip, research your destination, plan, and make sure you don't overspend. Essentially, be responsible.

But also remember that it will be a great trip if you go. If international travel isn't in your plans, you can channel this energy in other ways.

You may find that taking a class, joining a retreat, or doing a short course provides similar benefits. These things can also open your heart and mind, and you never know who you might meet.

Attending a spiritual retreat can be especially beneficial, as Jupiter in Taurus also carries a strong spiritual energy for you.

You may find yourself opening yourself up to new ideas spiritually or diving deeper into understanding who you really are.

The spiritual journey is truly endless, as we always come to new perceptions and awakenings of life and our role in it. Jupiter in Taurus could really see you travel to new depths, and these new depths could open your intuition and psychic abilities in ways you've never experienced before.

There is so much untapped potential in our minds, and Jupiter in Taurus will help you access it.

This is also a powerful time to read, learn, absorb new information, and maintain a student's mindset. Even in subjects where you feel like an expert, you may surprise yourself when you shift to a student mindset and see things from a beginner's lens. In fact, if there's something you want to improve on, and a skill you want to really polish in your life, going back to square one would be a fantastic way to use this energy.

It may sound a bit tedious, but you'll learn a lot and be in a much more powerful place of knowledge than you were before. Try it.

If you want to be good at something, Jupiter in Taurus is paving the way, and this is a good technique to try. Jupiter is helping you become the master.

So, think about an area of your life that you would like to master, and remember that you have all the cosmic support on your side to learn it and be the best at it.

Also important is that for you Jupiter has the potential to trigger legal problems. This may not resonate with you, but if it does, you may need to deal with mountains of paperwork and sort through all the finer details.

It might be hard work, but Jupiter will be on your side, making sure everything is managed fairly and equitably. You may even find that you are owed some unexpected money. Jupiter can bring surprises like that, and with the addition of Uranus to Taurus as well, you might find some pleasant surprises along the way.

Of course, while Jupiter is the ruler of abundance and can bring that to our path, he also rules over debts. This legal situation, or some fees or fines, may cross your path and require you to let go of some well-earned funds.

But keep in mind that money is simply an exchange of energy, and what you spin around will come back. You may even want to work with the mantra: for every dollar I give, three come my way.

This affirmation can help you shift to a positive mindset, especially if you have some unexpected or large bills piling up on you during this time.

Jupiter in Taurus is also fantastic if you are a student or have decided to go back to school.

As I mentioned earlier, higher education is very advantageous under this energy. In addition to enlightening and sharpening your mind, you may also find the school environment very inspiring.

You can meet people who open your eyes or discover a teacher you really resonate with.

This is a very expansive time for you mentally, and being in a school environment, especially one that inspires you, seems to be a good way to channel some of this energy.

If you work in education, Jupiter in Taurus may also be favorable for you. This would be a fantastic time to advance your career and pursue greater opportunities.

You may find an opportunity in your lap.

Pay attention around April-May 2024, as during this time there could be some volatility as Jupiter aligns closer to Uranus.

You can find things that reach a breaking point or something that comes to your head right now, trust whatever it is that falls, and don't be in a hurry to fix things.

Let the pieces fall where they can, let the dust settle and then evaluate your next steps. Ancient astrologers considered Jupiter the lucky planet as it always shone and brought gifts so even if something shakes in your life during this time, chances are it is simply paving the way for greater abundance in the future.

Another gift that Jupiter in Taurus will bring you is a greater ease when it comes to thinking positively. Jupiter will make it easier for you to see the positives and focus on the good things. You can help this by being aware of your thoughts and trying to stay in a lighter mood.

Jupiter also helps us see the big picture, and sometimes when we focus on the big picture, it allows us to shake off the unnecessary anxieties and stresses of the day and see what's important.

Allow Jupiter to work with your mind in this way. Adopt this way of thinking and you will see how Jupiter guides you to become a more optimistic thinker.

Who is Libra?

Dates: September 23 - October 22

Day: Friday

Color: Light green, light blue

Element: Air

Compatibility: Aries, Gemini, Aquarius, Sagittarius

Symbol:

Modality: Cardinal

Polarity: Male

Ruling planet: Venus

House: 7

Metal: Copper

Quartz: Lapis lazuli, Sapphire, Malachite

Constellation: Libra

What does Libra mean?

The legend of Libra is related to the Greek goddess Astrea, guardian of the rays of the powerful god Zeus. He advocated peace, and detested discord. represented by the constellation of Virgo.

This sign is symbolized by plates of the scales of justice, held by Astrea, daughter of Prudence and Modesty, goddess of justice, and innocence. Astrea symbolizes harmony and balance in everything and is depicted blindfolded, represented by impartiality,

Venus, The Ruling Planet of Taurus

Venus is the Goddess of Love. Venus rules the signs of Libra and Taurus. Venus is related to two main areas of our life: love and money. Love and Money really is a simplistic interpretation of Venus. Venus rules what we value, and the pleasure of life. Grace, charm, and beauty are ruled by Venus. Through Venus, we can know our tastes, pleasures, artistic inclinations, and the things that make us happy.

Predictions for Libra

For **Libra** Jupiter in Taurus could be a challenging location as it will guide you to see your financial situation in a new way.

You can be hit with some hard truths, or you may be in a situation where you need to invest more wisely or use your money smarter.

If you're married and your partner handles most of the finances, or if you have a money manager you trust, you may need to pay a little closer attention. You may even be in the situation where you have more money than you're used to and need to quickly learn how to manage it better and put it to work for you.

Understanding your finances is important here, and the Universe is preparing you to make this one of your core lessons with Jupiter in Taurus. It sounds a bit depressing, but learning how to manage money and your finances can keep you in a good position for the rest of your life.

And that's what Jupiter in Taurus is all about. It's about creating a strong environment for you to thrive, not just for today but for the rest of your life. Money is both a fortunate and unfortunate part of our reality in this dimension.

We need it to survive, and having enough can guarantee us a freedom that is hard to ignore. Gaining access to greater wealth can sometimes feel like something elusive that only certain people understand, but that's a convenient mindset drilled into us by those who prefer money to remain a mystery.

Working to heal your relationship with money is also connected to this transit. You may need to overcome your beliefs about money. "The money is dirty." "It's selfish to want more money." "I can't afford this." -If you think positively, you will always be provided-. -Not enough for everyone etc.

While there might be some truth to these claims, they are not absolute truths. We need to take a balanced approach to our relationship with money, and that's what you're being asked to do.

You are being called to question your own beliefs and values around money and see how they are serving you or holding you back.

You should take a moment to write down ten of your core beliefs when it comes to money and reflect on your list.

How many of these beliefs are rooted in scarcity versus abundance? Then dig a little deeper and ask yourself where these beliefs come from. Sometimes we can hold a belief as our truth until we challenge it and realize that we are holding on to someone else's beliefs that no longer apply to our current reality.

Work with this list as Jupiter travels through Taurus. You even think about what you want your beliefs to be and should put them somewhere as a reminder.

Learning about the practicality of money is also a good step because when you understand how it all works, you can start to feel more confident and balanced in your approach. Reading books, watching videos on YouTube, or even taking a money management course are some of the ways you can start learning and improving your knowledge about finance and investing.

There is a lot of power here to enter greater abundance, but you must do the work first!

As Jupiter aligns with Uranus in early 2024, you may find some unexpected money on your way. In fact, this location of Jupiter that you have on your chart is related to winning the lottery. Not that I am advising you to play the lottery, but there is some luck on your side, and you may come across some unexpected funds.

If you have some antique or collectible jewelry, you should be ready to part with it because Jupiter in Taurus can also help you find the perfect buyer and get a good price.

As with anything, you should do your research and be methodical, especially when Taurus is involved. But you have some good aspects on your side to making some money, not necessarily from your income, but from other alternative means.

This is also a good time to organize your will or to secure your assets in case of an emergency. It's never comfortable to think about these things, but with Jupiter in this location, it's a good time to deal with it.

Jupiter in Taurus will also expand your thoughts and feelings around your sexuality. You may be drawn to approach your sexuality in a different way, to become more intimate with your own body, or to understand what prevents you from connecting with others in a more intimate way. Jupiter is the planet of expansion, so your ideas about yourself and how you feel as a sexual being can be revised.

Many of us carry shame around our sexuality, but if you feel called, this could be your chance to let go of all that and step into greater freedom.

And finally, Jupiter in Taurus is going to be a spiritual location for you. While you're going to be questioning your relationship with money and what money means to you, your journey is likely to take you much deeper than this.

All your beliefs and values that are tied to your relationship with money are going to come to the surface, guiding you to make changes and reshape your relationship with abundance in all areas of your life. You may be thinking about your self-esteem and how open you are to receiving. You may have felt that you don't deserve certain things, or that certain things are for others, but now you may realize that you are just as deserving.

What once felt like it wasn't for you, or something that just other people did, you can now feel like a real perspective for you. Life is expanding. Life is showing you that you are worthy and that you deserve. Stay open to these ideas.

Expand your beliefs about yourself and what you thought was possible. You deserve it.

Who is Scorpio?

Dates: October 24 - November 22

Day: Tuesday

Color: Black, Dark Blue, Red

Element: Water

Compatibility: Taurus, Pisces

Symbol: ♏

Modality: Fixed

Polarity: Feminine

Ruling planet: Pluto and Mars

Home: 8 Death and Sex

Metal: iron

Quartz: Emerald, Onyx, Tourmaline

Constellation: Scorpion

What does Scorpio mean?

The legend associated with Scorpio involves the god Orion and the goddess Artemis. On one occasion, the presumptuous and rude Orion boasted that he was a superior hunter and that he would kill all the animals that lived on Earth to prove it.

Artemis, the goddess of the hunt, was very much in love with him and did not intend to prevent him. This infuriated Apollo, Orion's twin brother who, with the help of Gaia, the deity divinity of Earth created a cruel scorpion to lynch him.
The two fought and the scorpion won. In gratitude for his action in making impossible the disappearance of all animals, Zeus glorified him, placing him in the sky as the constellation of Scorpio.

Pluto, The Ruling Planet of Scorpio

Pluto in astrology, destroys to transform and regenerate what was destroyed. It is related to those drastic changes that move structures and generate indestructible changes in the world. It is linked to sex, mysteries, secrets, loans, debts, and power.

Predictions for Scorpio

Scorpio, Jupiter in Taurus is here to expand your heart and clear any damage or debris left from any distress.

Mistrust, trauma, and attachment issues, all these relationship issues are going to be on the table with Jupiter here.

And while some healing work is required, as well as some deepening, you'll find yourself going through a cleanse.

When you step out on the other side, you'll feel freer, more open, and connected to what your heart desires.

Jupiter is the planet of expansion, so think of it expanding into the center of your heart, helping you dislodge any unhealthy attachments that may have been trapped there. With the center of your heart expanded, Jupiter can also help you overcome any blockages and barriers that prevent you from making deeper connections with others.

Not only in your romantic relationships, but in all the relationships you have. As a Scorpio, you are particularly good at digging deep and down to the thick of your shadow, but with Jupiter, there is lightness.

You may find that you are able to achieve the same healing without having to drag away all the weeds because Jupiter allows us to see the positives more easily.

Ancient astrologers considered Jupiter the planet of gifts, as its energy allows us to see the gifts around us and within us with greater awareness. Not all healing journeys have to be these painful, long, and lengthy processes of excavation and processing. Sometimes they can be simple and light, and that's the tone Jupiter gives you.

This lightness will be especially welcome when you arrive at the Full Moon Lunar Eclipse in Taurus on October 28, 2023. This eclipse is part of a cycle you've been working with since November 2021.

Since this time, eclipses have all fallen on Scorpio (your sign) and Taurus, your opposite sign. These eclipses have been giving you training in all areas of your life, but now this cycle ends, and the last eclipse in this series will be this eclipse of October 2023.

As you near the end, the feeling of cleanliness will increase. Jupiter's work will intensify, and you might even be left with the feeling of being reborn.

With Jupiter in this corner of your chart, you will be able to maximize the blessings and teachings of this cycle of Eclipses and come out on the other side with a much healthier and more balanced approach to all the relationships in your life. It almost feels like a karmic cleansing where all your old habits and relationship patterns are over and are being reborn into something healthier than you are today.

Relationships are often complicated, and communication is one of the biggest obstacles.

Most of us are not taught how to connect and communicate with others. We simply grope our way through, learning as we go along, and sometimes get caught up in repetitive patterns we've inherited from our childhood conditioning.

Jupiter in Taurus is here to bring some revelations to your relationships and your communication style. It will help you clean up and release toxic patterns and behaviors, but it will also help you replace them with some positive ones.

Jupiter in Taurus could also bring a lucky relationship into your life. This doesn't have to be a romantic partner, although it can be. It can also be a teacher, mentor, manager, or agent who comes into your life and helps push you further. This person can also teach you how to trust again, how to connect again, and how it feels to be in an equal partnership with someone.

Very often, we may find ourselves in these relationship dynamics that can be a power struggle or can leave us feeling powerless.

We can also find relationships where we must take charge and we can never let our guard down completely because we are trusted so much.

Regardless of the dynamics and attachment styles that have been developing in your life, Jupiter in Taurus is here to bring some stability and ease.

It's here to calm the waters and help you reconnect with what's enormously important to you in your relationships. In fact, when working with this energy, it's good to ask yourself: What does a healthy relationship mean to you? How does it feel to be in a healthy relationship with a partner or otherwise? Being in a healthy relationship is always connected to your ability to set boundaries.

Boundaries are important as they set the law about how we want to be treated and what we are willing to tolerate. Our limits may vary from person to person, but often, we have some limits that apply to everyone.

This can be a good opportunity to check your limits. Are you defending them? Are they letting you suffocate or feeling taken advantage of you?

These questions would be helpful in guiding you to navigate where changes need to be made or where you need to be more assertive.

Jupiter on Taurus is also a fantastic position if you work in a commission-based business or if you have a job that requires you to connect with different clients. You could find more clients on your way, or if you work in the concert industry, this could also be a very lucrative time for you. If you're looking for a new agent or manager in your field of work, Jupiter in Taurus can also come in handy and can send a great match to your form.

Of course, you may have to do the hard work exposing yourself out there and getting the presentations. If you are looking to get married or take your relationship to the next level, Jupiter in Taurus is also a positive omen and indicates that your marriage will expand not only your heart, but also your world.

You can also benefit from this energy by choosing to level up a relationship in your life. For example, if it is a romantic couple, you can move in together. If it's with a teacher, you may decide to enroll in their individual coaching program.

If it's with an agent or manager, you can decide to sign an exclusive contract with them or add them to an agreement you're working on.

Work through whatever baggage is holding you back, keep it light, and then trust your instincts when it comes to leaning on others.

Who is Sagittarius?

Dates: November 23 - December 21

Day: Thursday

Color: blue-purple, green, and white

Element: fire

Compatibility: Libra, Gemini, Leo, and Aries

Symbol: ♐

Modality: mutable

Polarity: male

Ruling planet: Jupiter

House: 9

Metal: Tin

Quartz: Turquoise and Topaz

Constellation: Sagittarius

What does Sagittarius mean?

Mythology associates Sagittarius with the pious and tender centaur Chiron, half man, and half horse.

Chiron was intelligent, kind, and erudite. One day, when trying to control other centaurs who were creating trouble, Heracles, son of Zeus, accidentally struck Chiron with an arrow.

When he found him wounded with his poisoned arrows, Hercules felt much regret because, although Chiron was immortal, he suffered from pain.

Seeing his suffering, Prometheus, a heroic demigod, helped him, raising him to the heavens as the constellation of Sagittarius.

Jupiter, the ruling planet of Sagittarius

Jupiter, in Astrology, Jupiter is a planet of abundance, tolerance and expansiveness. The first of the social planets.

Jupiter seeks discernment through knowledge, it is a planet of purpose, and possibilities.

Predictions for Sagittarius

For **Sagittarius**, Jupiter moving into Taurus will keep you busy. Expect more projects to come your way and for your book to fill up a little more. Life will feel like you're moving at a faster pace, enjoy the ride.

But also remember that it will be important to stay on top of your limits and routine. In fact, creating a solid routine and honoring your limits will be your secret weapon as you travel through Jupiter in Taurus energy.

Stick to your boundaries, make sure you don't overfill your plate, and maintain a sense of structure and routine that helps you manage your day more efficiently.

If you work as a Freelancer, it is likely that Jupiter in Taurus will bring you a variety of projects. You may also find opportunities to speak your way, or you may be asked to promote your products and services at a large event.

There are plenty of opportunities here to promote yourself and what you do, so be sure to expose yourself and take advantage of these opportunities when they arrive! If you haven't already, this would be a great time to increase your social media, and really promote and share everything you offer.

If you don't work as a freelancer, this energy could manifest itself in taking on a big project. It could be at work or even inside the home. This great project could be lucrative for you in some way.

At work, this project could boost your reputation and even get you online for a promotion.

At home, this project could add value to your property or help you clean up things you can sell for extra income.

There is a sense of abundance flowing your way coming from this project opportunity. With so much going on, and all this energy fluttering around your chart, you have fantastic potential to get things done, move and change your life in powerful directions, make things happen.

When movement flows like this, great things tend to happen when you run with it. While I love all this activity that's flowing, and I encourage you to use it, you'll need to be mindful not to overdo it to the point where your health suffers.

If that's the case, and if the movement proves too much for you, Jupiter in Taurus can have the opposite effect, making you feel beaten.

The charge of energy rushing into your zodiac area will propel you forward or blow a fuse, wiping out what little energy you had left in the tank.

In some cases, you may find yourself oscillating through both states. You may go through periods of feeling turned on and motivated, and then go back to feeling lethargic and in need of rest.

If you're feeling lethargic or even lazy under this energy, take it as a sign that your body needs some time and space to catch up and recover!

Having Jupiter on Taurus is extremely helpful in restoring your body, so use it to your advantage!

Jupiter's earthly, grounded energy in Taurus will help your fiery mind slow down, recover, and be available for the simple things.

In fact, Jupiter in Taurus is a fantastic time to bring your consciousness to your lower energy centers, because they are the roots that ground us, give us stability, and help us stay in an even mental space. Especially if you find yourself swinging high and then low, Jupiter in Taurus will help you level things out, allowing you to take a more balanced approach and avoid extremes.

A quick way to land your energy is to walk barefoot on the grass. While you're there, bend your knees slightly and inhale and exhale, imagining that you are breathing in the energy of the earth.

Exercises like this can help balance your energetic body and keep you in stronger alignment. It will prevent you from feeling the effects of exhaustion or anxiety that can sometimes come when you have a lot on your plate.

Jupiter in Taurus is also a good reminder to focus on what brings you joy, and this is especially true if you find yourself busy. It's like that Zen saying: "If you don't have time to meditate for one hour a day, you should meditate for two." A busy mind that can't devote time to meditation is a disorganized mind that needs more meditation. I know an hour is a long time, but even just 5-10 minutes of meditation or self-care time every day can have a powerful effect on your nervous system.

Don't get so busy that you can't enjoy what really matters to you. Look at yourself if you start saying things like, "I don't have enough time for that—This is a scarcity thought and a sign that you need to slow down and prioritize your schedule better.

You may even need to outsource or lean on others for help. Sometimes it's not the number of things we need to do, but the emotional charge of those things that can also overwhelm us and make us feel even more overloaded.

Jupiter in Taurus will be here to guide you on the best way to manage your time and energy levels. You just need to get the ball rolling. Don't forget, Jupiter is your ruling planet, so it's always on the lookout for you!

Use your energy in Taurus to create more structure and stability, especially in your daily routine.

As far as your health is concerned, along with treating burnout, Jupiter in this position can sometimes exacerbate health issues you've ignored or gone unchecked.

During this 12-month period, make it a priority to address any symptoms or health issues.

Jupiter in Taurus can also inspire changing your diet and exercise routine.

There are so many voices in the wellness space with great ideas and things to try, but at the end of the day, you must listen to what's right and best for your body, and thankfully,

Jupiter in Taurus will let that voice speak loudly so you can hear it. Listen and connect with your body, listen to the wisdom it shares, because it will guide you.

By the time Jupiter is preparing to finish its journey on Taurus, hopefully you'll be in a place where you feel more grounded and structured with your daily routine and schedule, and more confident and energized in your mind, body, and soul. That is the blessing that Jupiter in Taurus can bring you.

Who is Capricorn?

Dates: December 22 - January 20

Day: Saturday

Color: Black, Terracotta

Element: earth

Compatibility: Taurus, Virgo, Pisces, and Cancer

Symbol: ♑

Modality: Cardinal

Polarity: Feminine

Ruling planet: Saturn

House: 10

Metal: Lead

Quartz: Agate, Black Tourmaline, Fluorite, Garnet

Constellation: Capricorn

What does Capricorn mean?

In mythology Capricorn is associated with the goat with a fish tail, and the body of a goat that lived near the sea and was admired for being an intelligent creature. Bred by Cronos, the god of time, this sea goat had the ability to manipulate time.

This goat suffered with great sadness as all her children moved away from the sea and swam to the beach to stay on dry land.

With the passage of time, their children lost their tails, intelligence, the ability to live in the sea, that is, they transformed into normal goats. To make it impossible for this to happen, the sea goat invested the time and informed his children of the fate and karma that awaited them on Earth, but his effort was zero. His children continued to swim to Earth and left the sea for good.

Desolate the sea goat asked Cronus to annul his immortality, but instead, he was placed in the sky as a constellation of Capricorn. From the sky he could see his children, even when playing on the highest top of the mountains.

Saturn, The Ruling Planet of Capricorn

Saturn is associated with restrictions and limitations. Where Jupiter expands, Saturn contracts. Although Saturn's themes seem depressing, Saturn brings structure and meaning to our world. Saturn knows the limits of time and reminds us of our limits, responsibilities, and commitments. It brings structures into our lives.

Predictions for Capricorn

For Capricorn, Jupiter in Taurus is a romantic place, as it will activate the part of your card related to love, romance, and play!

This is one of the best locations for Jupiter, so get excited and remember that you have beautiful cosmic support on your side! In fact, you deserve this soft, light, poetic energy, as

Pluto has been giving you great cosmic training for the past 20 years or so.

While Pluto isn't quite finished in Capricorn, it's nearing the end of the journey and most of the work Pluto had in store for you is now ending and ending. What better way to celebrate than to have Jupiter in the part of your chart that will activate and expand, romance, love, and play.

With Jupiter on Taurus, you will feel more cheerful and even feel the need to take a break from work and relax.

Pluto in your sign may have left you feeling a little heavy, but with Pluto on its way out and Jupiter in this position of your chart, a lightness will return.

Observe this change in your life and recognize how it inspires you to focus on the positive aspects of things more easily.

The stereotype paints Capricorn as the workaholic of the zodiac, but as Jupiter moves into Taurus, you may finally feel the need to relax, and enjoy the efforts of your job.

You may feel the need to slow down, stop, and be available to play so you don't miss out on life's fun.

Jupiter on Taurus will deliver the message, but it will be up to you to make the changes that are needed. You've been working too hard, or just putting too much stress or unnecessary pressure on yourself.

It's not even what's happening in your external environment that's weighing you down, but it's in your internal environment.

Sometimes, our minds can run in overdrive, making everything seem more difficult and important than it needs to be. With Jupiter in Taurus here, you are being guided to slow down, relax your mind, and practice some stillness.

When your mind slows down, life can slow down, and when that happens, you tend to notice the beauty around you.

In addition to slowing down and enjoying some pleasures, Jupiter entering Taurus is also fantastic for your love life. If you're single, this is one of the best years to meet someone special.

If that's important to you, put yourself in the dating scene. Even though the whole process may seem tedious and difficult, you have luck and the abundance of Jupiter on your side.

If you're in a relationship, this would be a wonderful year to take your relationship to the next level, renew your vows, or just make more time for each other.

And if you're not interested in relationships right now, channel this energy into the best love there is: self-love!

This energy of love can also reach your children or pets. Enjoy their company more, or if you're thinking about starting a family, Jupiter on Taurus can be an especially fertile place for you.

On a deeper healing level, Jupiter is the planet of expansion, and what is expanding here is your heart and your feelings of joy and pleasure. This is an opportunity for you to open your heart more widely, to let go of heavy habits that no longer serve you, and to adopt a more open and compassionate way of being.

You can be slow to trust and slow to open, especially when it comes to your intimate relationships.

But Jupiter is here, on your side, helping you feel more tender, open, and vulnerable. Allow some of the pains and shames of the past to fade, so that your heart can open deeper.

If you've been feeling stuck in your heart chakra, this is a wonderful opportunity to do some cleansing.

A blocked heart chakra can manifest as feeling disconnected, lonely, or isolated. It can also manifest as a lack of belonging or difficulty opening to others.

It may be hard for you to feel your feelings, or you may have a hard time allowing yourself to get close to someone.

In your outside world, this can manifest as finding unavailable partners or having difficulty staying in long-term relationships.

You can also bury yourself in your work or responsibilities to distract yourself. If you resonate with any of this, know that Jupiter in Taurus will guide you to break free and open.

Research ways to open your heart chakra but remember that sometimes simply setting the intention can be a powerful start.

You can do this through a quick meditation practice. Just close your eyes, place your hand over your heart, and imagine that you are inhaling and exhaling from your heart. As if your heart is your nose, taking every breath and releasing every breath. Do 40 breaths like that. Then take your hand and tap gently against your chest, awakening the energy and inviting more heart-centered feelings into your life.

This is a simple meditation that you can adjust to meet your needs and what you feel in the moment. There are also many other heart chakras opening exercises you can try, so feel free to experiment with what works best for you.

Along with love and romance as a theme for you, Jupiter in Taurus is also a highly creative energy and the perfect time to bring a more creative touch to everything you do and your surroundings.

If you've wanted to take a more creative role at work, Jupiter in Taurus will be on your side, helping you forge a path to get there. Alternatively, if you already work in a creative field, you might see a brilliant and lucrative project opportunity on your way. You can also make your own success by authoring that book or making that work of art.

Creative work is likely to lead you to success under this transit, so don't stop! You can also feel more creative in general, and this can be expressed in your surroundings and in the clothes you wear.

This would be a good time to update your wardrobe or to experiment with a new hairstyle. Do what you need to do to feel more beautiful in your own skin.

Jupiter in Taurus is truly a beautiful, joyful, and fun place for you, and I hope you can use this energy in your life.

This is your chance to let go of your hair, loosen yourself, release some control, give up some of your responsibilities, and focus on joy. Sow small seeds of joy into your daily routine and watch Jupiter expand it for you.

Who is Aquarius?

Dates: January 21 to February 19

Day: Saturday

Color: Purple

Element: Air

Compatibility: Leo, Libra. Sagittarius

Symbol: ♒

Modality: Fixed

Polarity: Male

Ruling planet: Uranus and Saturn

House: 11

Metal: Chrome

Quartz: Amethyst, pomegranate

Constellation: Aquarius

What does Aquarius mean?

The myth of Aquarius is the story of Ganymede, a beautiful prince of Troy. One day, while Ganymede was tending his father's flocks, he was spotted by Zeus who was mesmerized by their beauty.

Transfiguring himself into an eagle, he imprisoned the young man and took him to Mount Olympus, transforming him into his slave and lover.

Ganymede was the water carrier of the gods, offering them drinks when they asked for them. Ganymede revealed himself to his position as a servant and Zeus, instead of rebuking him, gave him immortality by placing him in the stars as the constellation Aquarius.

This story reminds us that chaos and rebellion are imperative when fighting for freedom.

Uranus, The Ruling Planet of Aquarius

Astrologically, Uranus is associated with technology, and electronic devices, speed, electricity, freedom, revolutions, and sudden changes of order. It relates to new ways of thinking and inspires solutions.

Predictions for Aquarius

For Aquarius, as Jupiter enters Taurus, it will hit a sacred angle of your chart, putting you in one of the best positions to breathe the healing and restorative optimism that Jupiter can provide.

Ancient astrologers considered Jupiter a beneficial force in our lives, and it was painted as the lucky planet.

Jupiter in Taurus will be radiating some good fortune on your path, allowing you to appreciate the gifts that surround you and live within you. In fact, as Jupiter travels through Taurus, it will remind you of your talents, the things you're good at and help you feel that confidence boost to express who you really are. Think of Jupiter in Taurus as something that is activating and awakening those pearls of wisdom, those jewels of natural talent that are buried within you.

Jupiter in Taurus will help you realize your potential and focus on all the things you are gifted with and good at. You may be reading I'm thinking I'm not gifted at all,

But Jupiter is here to challenge that belief. Jupiter in Taurus will draw out your given blessings, helping you to activate and connect with the divine light that lives within you.

Part of this process involves boosting your confidence and getting into more of who you really are. Jupiter in Taurus can offer some healing, helping you peel off the layers that prevent you from absolutely loving yourself and stepping into the fullness of your potential.

While healing work may sound a bit depressing, especially since you've had so much cosmic activity in your zodiac sign, this healing will be gentle and emerge from a place of light rather than darkness.

We don't always have to travel through the depths to heal. Sometimes it can come from a simpler place, and that's what's offered here.

Jupiter in Taurus offers a way to get to know you better, love yourself more, and know that your energy is a gift to this world. Each of us has our own spark and light, and it's up to us to follow that and bring it into everything we do.

As Jupiter in Taurus hits this sacred angle in your chart, it will guide you so that you can become a more authentic version of yourself. You may be wondering, who am I really?

You can also get a boost of courage to finally take charge and do something you've always wanted to do. Instead of thinking about self-limiting beliefs or avoiding moving forward, Jupiter in Taurus can help you see opportunities rather than closed doors. The more abundant you can be with the way you think and the words you use, the easier it will be for Jupiter in Taurus to infuse its magic into your life and unlock some of the natural inspiration that lives within you.

In fact, by the time Jupiter finishes traveling through Taurus, hopefully, you'll have identified some new gifts and talents or leaned on your existing gifts and talents, and you'll be able to create some abundance from them.

For example, you may find that a hobby you love to do, or are particularly good at, turns into a business opportunity. Or, a natural gift you possess, such as your intuition, or being naturally good with plants or animals, can become something lucrative and abundant for you.

This energy is about focusing on your natural gifts and expressing them in the world. These natural gifts could very well lead to income or simply bring a sense of expansion and wonder to your world. Along with Jupiter helping to unravel more of your natural gifts, it will also activate household affairs.

You may want to move or redesign your living space. If you decide to renew right now, just make sure you have some extra funds stashed away, as there's a chance it could end up costing more than you expected.

Buying a property can also be on your mind; If that's the case, it could be an excellent investment.

Of course, you should do proper research, but the property you buy could bring you a lot of abundance. This abundance could come from the final sale price, but it could also come from the inspiration the new home offers you.

This new home provides a good home office that brings new inspiration and allows you to do your job more effectively, helping to bring more monetary abundance that way.

If you want to sell a property, there is also great potential for you to be presented with a lucrative deal. So, if you've been thinking about doing this, Jupiter in Taurus may be a good time to act.

Feeling inspired by where you live is important and something Jupiter in Taurus wants to offer you, so work with this energy and see where it takes you. Remember that Jupiter will be on your side to create a grounded base wherever you choose to live.

Family matters can also arise with Jupiter in this position. You may need to be there for a family member, or you may feel tied to family commitments in some way.

Your family unit may also be expanding through your marriage or someone in your family who has a child.

You may also want to be closer to your family during this time and repair old wounds that prevent you from feeling comfortable with your family. Family wounds are exceedingly difficult to navigate, as they tend to come with a lot of drama. For many of us, many of our family wounds are also connected to past lives, making them even more complex to understand.

If you have family wounds that come to the surface during this time, know that Jupiter in Taurus is helping you create a sense of stability, so you know where you stand and can set the perfect boundaries so that harmony and peace can be maintained.

As family matters are so complex, and there is a chance that they will rise under this energy, seeking support from a therapist or other professional may be a good idea.

Jupiter in Taurus offers grounding, but you may need to take it a step further by seeking support to help you stay in this state of being.

Therapy and other modalities can be highly effective in not only guiding you through any family wounds, but also helping you boost your confidence and bring out those buried gems hidden inside you.

Your talents are coming to the surface; Embrace them, embrace all that you are, and remember that any family healing will only help guide you toward deeper, higher truth.

Who is Pisces?

Dates: February 19 - March 20

Day: Thursday

Colors: Sea green, blue and violet.

Element: Water

Compatibility: Cancer, Scorpio, Taurus, Virgo

Symbol: ♓

Modality: Mutable

Polarity: Feminine

Ruling planet: Neptune and Jupiter

House: 12

Metal: Nickel

Quartz: Amethyst lapis lazuli,

Constellation: Pisces

What does Pisces mean?

According to legend Pisces is related to Aphrodite, goddess of beauty, and her son Eros the divinity of love).

One day, the Earth goddess sent the mighty monster Typhon to Mount Olympus to attack the gods. To protect themselves from their attacks, the gods were transmuted into animals. Aphrodite and Eros were bathing in the Euphrates River and did not hear the howls of warning.

When Typhon suddenly emerged from the waters, the two gods turned into Fishes to escape the fury of the ogre. Pisces was assigned the constellation Pisces to praise the salvation of love and beauty.

Neptune, The Ruling Planet of Pisces

Neptune is a planet that acts subtly and mysteriously. He likes to undermine the ego and allows the individual to be diluted into the universal. It is synchronized with unconditional love and

It is mixed in culture and society. In the natal chart its position indicates themes the person does not see clearly and can be deceived, but it will also bring softness and inspiration to this area.

Predictions for Pisces

For Pisces, the last sign of the zodiac, Jupiter moving towards Taurus will bring many rewards and successes.

Jupiter is the planet of expansion, and it can expand a particular area of our chart.

The area that's ripe for expansion in your chart relates to your ability to communicate, connect, and share your story with the world. This means that Jupiter is going to push you into the spotlight. Your voice will become more powerful.

People will see you as an authority; You can even find yourself organizing conferences or hosting a popular podcast. Your voice is your key here, and Jupiter will guide you to use it in a purposeful way.

Even if you don't become a famous talk show host during this transit, Jupiter will guide you to find strength and power in your voice.

Your throat chakra will be activated, and when you can speak and communicate from a place of strength, courage, and truth, the benefits will be endless in all areas of your life, both professionally and personally.

To activate this energy and make it work for you, it will be important to start focusing on how you communicate with others and how you feel when it comes to speaking and sharing your truth. Are you hiding? Do you drown when a stranger starts a conversation with you? Will you say what you really mean, or will you nod your head to avoid conflict?

Take a moment to think about how you currently use your voice and then what you need to change. You even think of three or four things you can do to start changing the way you communicate and the thoughts that keep you from sharing what you really want to say.

On a broader level, Jupiter can also inspire you to share your story with the world on a platform like the internet or through a publication.

If you've ever had the idea of starting to author a book, Jupiter will be on your side, helping your voice to be transmitted clearly and strongly. You have a story to share, you have wisdom to share, and this is a fantastic time to talk.

Consider publishing that novel that's on your computer, publishing the first episode of a podcast, or that blog post.

Take some action, as you never know where it may take you and what will result from it.

Alternatively, this energy can help you become a coach, mentor, or expert in your profession. People will see you as an authority and hire you to listen to your advice and wisdom. If you've thought about moving into a coaching, mentoring, or coaching role, this would also be a fantastic time to explore any opportunity. You may even find an opportunity to do this as a side job to generate additional income.

If you have wanted to do a speaking event or practice public speaking, this energy is also very favorable and will help you get the courage to get on the podium and share your ideas.

On a deeper level, this energy is about helping you connect with the wisdom of your voice so you can realize your power and then share it with the world.

A creative story or idea is not good sitting in your head or unfinished on the computer; This is your chance to expose your ideas to the world, for the sole reason that people need to hear your story.

It may be one person, or it may be millions, but Jupiter in Taurus is all about speaking up and sharing your ideas and visions with the world around you. If you work in a humanitarian or non-profit field, this energy is also helpful, as you may find that more people start listening to what you have to say and help where assistance is really needed.

No matter your industry or how you decide to share your voice, Jupiter in Taurus will also boost your confidence. You may have had some setbacks lately, or maybe you've felt a lot of pressure.

Saturn moved into your sign in March 2023, and this can be a challenging energy to work with. Saturn is known as the Lord of Karma; It helps us take responsibility for our actions and the life we want to lead.

It can bring challenging situations our way, evaluating us and making us fight for what we truly desire and believe in.

If this resonates, it may let you know that Jupiter moving into Taurus will lighten this burden for you. Any heaviness brought by

Saturn has the potential to feel softer, and it will be easier for you to see the positives.

That is one of the benefits that Jupiter can bring; It can expand our minds, causing us to focus on the good things and the many gifts around us. Lately, you've been feeling a little depressed about yourself and your abilities.

You have felt that life still brings some setbacks, but Jupiter will guide you to focus on a more abundant mindset, allowing you to see the opportunities rather than the obstacles.

Jupiter will help others respect what you say, but in this process, you must also respect yourself. Do you trust and recognize how talented you are? Do you trust and recognize that you really have something worth sharing?

You are a highly creative soul, and your creative energies will be swimming high with Jupiter in Taurus, so use all of this to your advantage! As a water sign, you like to go with the current and ride the waves. Having an organized routine or structure may not suit your watery qualities.

However, with Saturn, a very earthly planetary force in your sign, and Jupiter in Taurus, another earth sign, a strong earth energy surrounds you, guiding you to create structure, order, and routine in your daily life.

Having a set routine may not work for you all the time, but with all this earthly energy in the cosmic heavens, you may find that life is easier when you have concrete plans in place each day. You may also find it easier to get things done and feel more aligned and focused.

If you tend to be a little scattered, this energy is a wonderful tonic to feel more grounded and centered. Try having a set schedule or some productivity tricks.

Having some structure is going to be beneficial and help you create more longevity around whatever success comes your way. In fact, with Jupiter on Taurus and Saturn in Pisces, this combination of energy can be a signature for lasting success and can help you create feelings of security.

Overall, Jupiter in Taurus will activate your voice and guide you to speak your truth. This is a very enriching time for you, but it will manifest slowly and gradually over the next 12 months.

It is Jupiter's hope that you come out of this journey more awake, confident, and confident in who you are and what you must share.

About the Authors

In addition to her astrological knowledge, Alina Rubi has an abundant professional education; She has certifications in Psychology, Hypnosis, Reiki, Bioenergetic Crystal Healing, Angelic Healing, Dream Interpretation and is a Spiritual Instructor. Rubi has knowledge of Gemology, which she uses to program stones or minerals and turn them into powerful Amulets or Talismans of protection.

Rubi has a practical and purposeful character, which has allowed him to have a special and integrating vision of several worlds, facilitating solutions to specific problems.

Alina writes the Monthly Horoscopes for the website of the American Association of Astrologers; you can read them on the site www.astrologers.com.

At this moment he writes a weekly column in the newspaper El Nuevo Herald on spiritual topics, published every Sunday in digital form and on Mondays in print. He also has a program and the Weekly Horoscope on the YouTube channel of this newspaper. His Astrological Yearbook is published every year in the newspaper -Diario las Américas-, under the column Rubi Astrologa.

Rubi has authored several articles on astrology for the monthly publication -Today's Astrologer-, has taught classes in Astrology, Tarot, Reading the hands, Crystal Healing, and Esotericism. She has weekly videos on esoteric topics on her YouTube channel: Rubi Astrologa. T

She has her own Astrology program broadcast daily through Flamingo T.V., she has been interviewed by several T.V. and radio programs, and every year her -Astrological Yearbook- is published with the horoscope sign by sign, and other interesting mystical topics.

She is the author of the books -Rice and Beans for the Soul- Part I, II, and III, a compilation of esoteric articles, published in English, Spanish, French, Italian and Portuguese. -Money for All Pockets-, -Love for All Hearts-, -Health for All Bodies, Astrological Yearbook 2021, Horoscope 2022, Rituals and Spells for Success in 2022,

Spells and Secrets, Astrology Classes, Rituals and Amulets 2023 and Chinese Horoscope 2023 all available in five languages: English, Italian, French, Japanese and German.

Rubi speaks English and Spanish perfectly, combining all her talents and knowledge in her readings. He currently resides in Miami, Florida.

For more information you can visit the website www.esoterismomagia.com

Alina A. Rubi is the daughter of Alina Rubi. She is currently studying psychology at Florida International University.

As a child she was interested in all metaphysical, esoteric, and practical subjects of astrology, and Kabbalah from the age of four. He has knowledge of Tarot, Reiki, and Gemology. She is not only the author, but editor together with her sister Angeline A. Rubi, of all the books published by her and her mother.

For more information you can contact her by email: rubiediciones29@gmail.com

Milton Keynes UK
Ingram Content Group UK Ltd.
UKHW020732291223
435170UK00014B/599